A SOLDIER'S LIFE IN

ROMAN TIMES

ROMAN TIMES

Fiona Corbridge

W
FRANKLIN WATTS
LONDON • SYDNEY

Illustrations by:
Mark Bergin
Giovanni Caselli
Chris Molan
Lee Montgomery
Peter Visscher
Maps by Hardlines

First published in 2006 by
Franklin Watts
338 Euston Road
London NW1 3BH

Franklin Watts Australia
Hachette Children's Books
Level 17/207 Kent Street
Sydney NSW 2000

Series editor: John C. Miles
Art director: Jonathan Hair

This book is based on
Going to War in Roman Times
by Moira Butterfield © Franklin Watts 2000.
It is produced for Franklin Watts
by Painted Fish Ltd.
Designer: Rita Storey

A CIP catalogue record
for this book is available
from the British Library

ISBN 0 7496 6491 6

Dewey classification: 355.00937

Printed in China

CONTENTS

THE ROMAN EMPIRE

The Romans were a people who came from the city of Rome (which they called Roma) in Italy (Italia). Rome started with a few huts between 1000 and 800 BCE. It gradually grew and grew.

Over the next thousand years, the Romans conquered (fought and took over) many countries. These became part of the Roman Empire.

Vallum Hadriani
(Hadrian's Wall)

Deva

Londinium

**BRITANNIA
(now Britain)**

Lutetia

**GAUL
(now Franc**

*OCEANUS ATLANTICUS
(Atlantic Ocean)*

Massilia

**HISPANIA
(now Spain)**

Italica

Carthago
Nova

Gades

 The Roman Empire

 Roman settlements (places where Romans lived)

Battles

A legend says that two brothers brought up by a wolf started the city of Rome

Romans were ruled by emperors. The first Roman emperor was Augustus

**Rome
600–500 BCE**
By this time, Rome had grown from a tiny settlement into a huge city.

**Julius Caesar
100–44 BCE**
Julius Caesar was a powerful Roman emperor. He fought many important battles.

**Claudians
30 BCE–CE 69**
Augustus started a dynasty called the Claudians.

The Roman army
The Romans had a big, strong army. They used it to take control of many countries. These countries became part of the Roman Empire. *This map shows the Roman Empire in CE 117, when it was at its largest and most powerful. It stretched from Britain to Egypt.*

GERMANIA (now Germany)

DACIA (now Romania)

ILLYRICUM

ITALIA (now Italy)

Salonae

THRACIA (now part of Turkey)

PONTUS EUXINUS (Black Sea)

Constantinople

ARMENIA

Roma

MACEDONIA (Greece)

Pergamum

SICILIA (now Sicily)

Athenae

Corinthus

Carthago

Syracusae

MESOPOTAMIA

Leptis Magna

JUDAEA

Petra

Alexandria

AFRICA

The Palace of Diocletian

The Roman Empire in CE 117
The Empire was at its largest when Emperor Trajan ruled.

The Empire splits, CE 286
The Empire was split into two parts – east and west – by Emperor Diocletian.

Fall of Rome, CE 410
German tribes destroyed the city of Rome. Constantinople became the new capital of the Empire.

LEGIONS

The Roman army was made up of groups of soldiers called legions. Each legion had a name and a fortress. There were about 30 legions around the Roman Empire.

A legion had commanders, officers and ordinary soldiers. There were also doctors, engineers and other workers.

STANDARDS
Each legion had its own standards – poles with badges on them.

A LEGION

There were about 6,000 men in a legion: 10 cohorts, horsemen and specialists

10 cohorts (a legion)

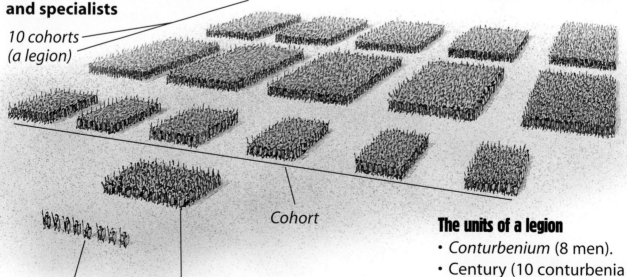

Cohort

Century

Conturbenium

Organizing the troops
The legion was made up of different units.

The units of a legion
- *Conturbenium* (8 men).
- Century (10 conturbenia – 80 men).
- Cohort (6 centuries – 480 men).
- Legion (10 cohorts).

AT THE TOP OF A LEGION

The legate and his six officers called tribunes all came from noble families in Rome. They only served in the army for a short time and then went to rule important provinces.

> *To become a soldier you had to be a boy aged eighteen or over. You had to be at least 1.7 metres tall and healthy.*

AT THE BOTTOM

A new recruit started as a legionary. He could work his way up to become a centurion, or even *praefectus castrorum*.

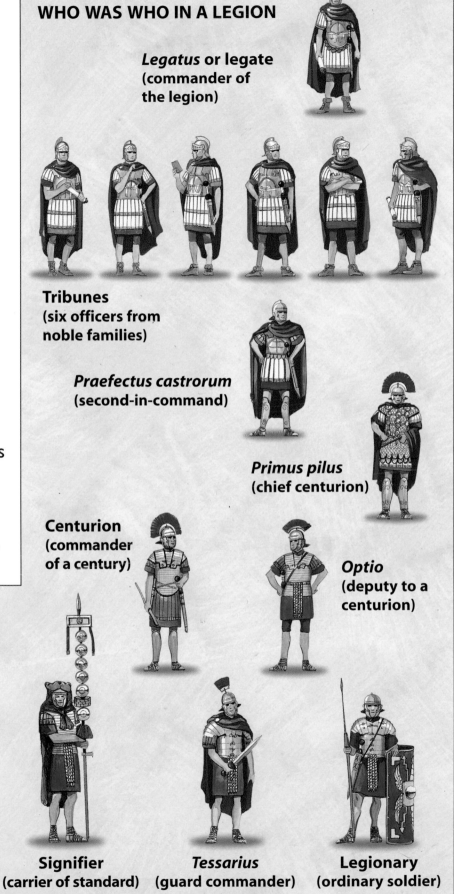

WHO WAS WHO IN A LEGION

Legatus or legate (commander of the legion)

Tribunes (six officers from noble families)

Praefectus castrorum (second-in-command)

Primus pilus (chief centurion)

Centurion (commander of a century)

Optio (deputy to a centurion)

Auxiliary (soldier who was not a Roman citizen)

Signifier (carrier of standard)

Tessarius (guard commander)

Legionary (ordinary soldier)

JOIN THE ARMY!

If you wanted to become a legionary, you had to go for an interview. The army only allowed men of good character to join. You had to agree to be a soldier for twenty-five years. You would be sent to a legion and asked to take an oath of loyalty (make a promise to be loyal) to the Roman emperor.

🔘 **I PROMISE . . .**
Soldiers raised one hand to take the oath of loyalty to the emperor.

ARMY PAY

Denarii

Why join?
Being a soldier was a good job. You learned skills and were well fed. You travelled with the legion to far-off lands. At the end of your career, you got a pension.

Pay
A legionary earned about 300 denarii (silver pieces) per year. The army kept some of this money for food, equipment, a pension and a funeral.

25 oysters cost 1 denarius

A shirt cost 25 denarii

Where the money went

Pension   *Spending*

Funeral   *Food and equipment*

Spending
Legionaries' pay did not go far. A new shirt cost about a month's pay.

LEARNING SKILLS

New recruits were taught skills that were useful to the army. They learned how to make roads and build things out of wood. They even had swimming lessons.

DAILY ROUTINE

Every day, recruits went to the parade ground to learn and rehearse marching patterns and battle formations. They also practised following officers' commands.

Manoeuvres
The army often went on manoeuvres. These were exercises for soldiers to practise what they had learnt. They went on long marches and overnight camping trips.

KILL!

Recruits learned to fight by attacking posts with wooden swords, javelins and shields made out of wicker.

A centurion watches troops in training

ARMOUR AND WEAPONS

All Roman soldiers wore a uniform and armour to protect them against being wounded in battle. This picture shows a legionary from CE 117, when the Roman Empire was at its most powerful.

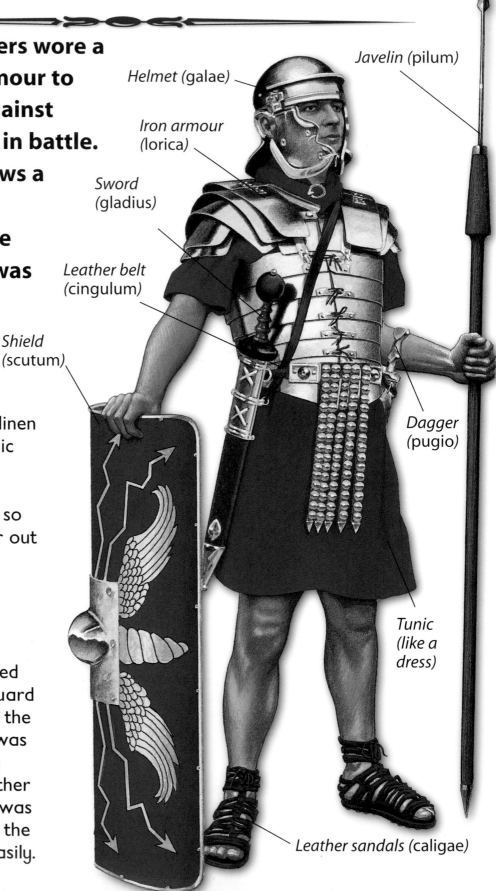

Helmet (galae)

Javelin (pilum)

Iron armour (lorica)

Sword (gladius)

Leather belt (cingulum)

Shield (scutum)

Dagger (pugio)

Tunic (like a dress)

Leather sandals (caligae)

⬤ TUNIC AND SANDALS

A legionary wore a linen undershirt and a tunic made of wool. His leather sandals had hobnails in the soles so they would not wear out on long marches.

⬤ ARMOUR

A metal helmet with cheek pieces protected the head. It had a guard to cover the back of the neck. Body armour was made of overlapping iron strips held together by leather straps. It was heavy but flexible so the soldier could move easily.

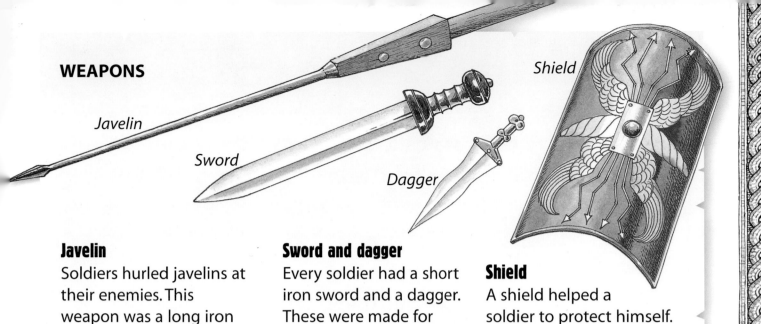

WEAPONS

Javelin

Sword

Dagger

Shield

Javelin
Soldiers hurled javelins at their enemies. This weapon was a long iron stick with a pointed tip and a wooden handle.

Sword and dagger
Every soldier had a short iron sword and a dagger. These were made for stabbing the enemy at close range.

Shield
A shield helped a soldier to protect himself. It was made from wood covered in leather or linen.

⊙ STANDARD-BEARERS

Every century in a legion had a soldier called a signifier to carry a standard. He wore a bearskin. The most important standard was the *aquila*. It had a golden eagle on it and was carried by the *aquilifer*.

Latin
The language of the Romans was Latin. The word for "golden eagle" was "aquila", which is where the name "aquilifer" comes from.

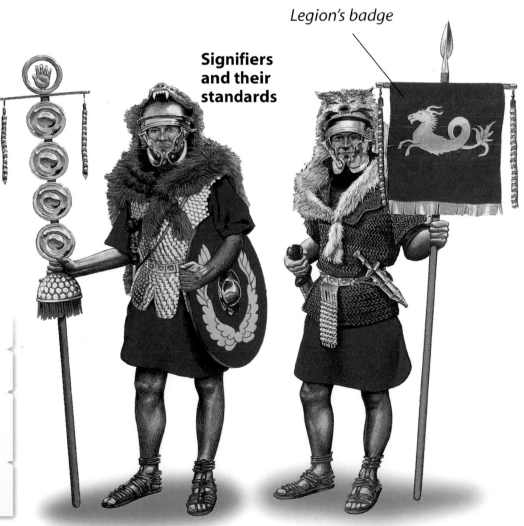

Signifiers and their standards

Legion's badge

AUXILIARIES

A legion also had soldiers called auxiliaries. They were men who had been born in other lands, and so were not Roman citizens. They wore a different uniform to the legionaries.

   Auxiliaries often had special skills, such as horse-riding and archery (using a bow and arrow).

Stabbing spear (hasta)

Chainmail

Oval shield

Auxiliary foot soldier

Auxiliary archer

Chainmail shirt made of metal links to protect the soldier

DIFFERENT TROOPS

There were different sorts of auxiliary troops. Light infantry soldiers had just a few weapons. Cavalry soldiers rode horses. Both were used as scouts (soldiers sent out to get information) and to go on patrol.

THE LIFE OF AN AUXILIARY

The Roman navy

Many Romans did not like going to sea. Auxiliaries who came from seaside villages made good crews for the Romans' ships.

Postings

Auxiliary units were often sent to work a long way from home so that they would not have to fight their own people.

Retirement

When an auxiliary came to the end of his career, he was awarded Roman citizenship. This was a great honour that he could pass on to his children.

THE CAVALRY

Auxiliary cavalry units were called the *ala*. Their soldiers learned to jump on to a moving horse, and to hit a target while galloping.

SHOWING OFF

Sometimes the cavalry put on riding displays for the rest of the legion. They wore decorated armour and golden helmets.

An auxiliary cavalryman

INSIDE A FORTRESS

The legion lived in a fortress. This was a group of buildings protected by thick walls. Soldiers lived in barracks and officers had houses. There were stores for food and equipment, workshops, bathhouses and a hospital.

There was usually a settlement outside the fortress with shops and taverns.

CENTURION

The centurion had rooms near to the barracks, so he could keep an eye on the 80 soldiers in his century.

Fireplace

Kitchen area

Bunk bed

Straw-filled mattress

Dice game

BARRACK ROOMS

Each conturbenium of eight men lived in one room. They had bunks to sleep on and a kitchen area. Here they could sleep, rest, play dice or clean their armour. They collected food rations from the stores to cook and eat there.

COOKING

The soldiers had a stove to cook on. It was a bit like a modern barbecue.

FORTS AND LOOKOUTS

A fort was smaller than a fortress. A cohort of 480 men could live in it.

The Romans also had lookout posts, where just a few soldiers lived and kept watch.

Camps
When soldiers were on a march and could not get back to the fortress, they made a camp and slept in tents.

A fortress

Gateway

Wall

Ditch

Barrack blocks

Sentry on duty

LIFE IN A FORTRESS

Bathhouse
Soldiers went to the bathhouse to swim and bathe. They could also have a massage.

Chores
Every day legionaries had to do chores such as sweeping their barrack room.

Family life
Soldiers could not marry but their families lived in the settlement outside the fortress.

ON THE MARCH

Legions marched with each rank in its place.

Soldiers moved from one place to another by marching. Their marching speed was about six kilometres an hour and they walked for five hours before having a rest. They had to carry their kit, weapons and armour. Each night they built a camp to sleep in, which they could defend if they were attacked.

Legionary on the march

A SOLDIER'S KIT
Each legionary carried his kit (equipment) on a pole. He had food, tools, cooking utensils and two stakes to help build a palisade (wooden wall) around the camp.

MAKING CAMP

The campsite
All campsites were made to the same plan. When a site had been chosen, a rectangle was marked out on the ground.

Digging
The soldiers dug a ditch and piled up the earth into a bank around the rectangle. Other soldiers stayed on guard.

Defences against attack
On top of the bank, soldiers made a palisade from the wooden stakes. Then they put up their tents in neat rows.

AMBUSH!

A legion had to be on its guard in case an enemy tried a surprise attack called an ambush. Scouts went ahead to keep a lookout. The troops marched with the commanders in the middle, and cavalry and infantry soldiers at the back. This made it easier to fight if they were ambushed.

British ambush
Britain was part of the Roman Empire. But some Britons fought against the Romans. In CE 60 they ambushed and killed part of a legion on its way to London.

LOST LEGIONS

In CE 9, three legions disappeared in the Black Forest in Germany. Nobody knew what had happened to them. Then later expeditions found piles of bones. All the soldiers had been killed. They were probably ambushed while building their camp.

FIGHTING BATTLES

Before a battle, a Roman army always lined up in order. Legionaries were at the front, with reserve troops behind them. Auxiliaries were on either side. This sort of careful planning helped the Romans to beat their enemies.

Lining up for battle

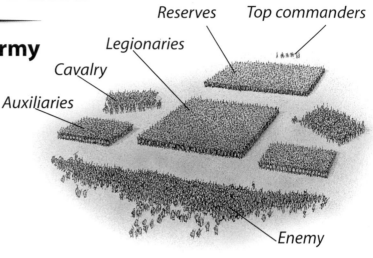

Reserves

Top commanders

Legionaries

Cavalry

Auxiliaries

Enemy

BATTLE FORMATIONS

Troops also lined up in different shapes, called formations, for battle.

BATTLE ORDERS

JAVELINS
Throw one, then march on and throw another.

AUXILIARIES
Fire slingshots, bows and arrows at the enemy.

STAB LOW
In hand-to-hand combat, stab with your sword.

SHIELD
Use your shield to bash upwards at the enemy.

LEFT-HANDED SOLDIERS
Fight together in a special section.

OBEY THE CENTURION
Do what you're told. If you don't, you'll be killed.

DIFFERENT FORMATIONS

Square

If a group of soldiers was surrounded, they stood in a square. Their shields made a wall. Soldiers on the outside stuck their javelins out.

Pig's head

The tortoise

To attack a fort, soldiers put their shields above their heads to protect themselves from missiles thrown from the walls by the enemy.

Square

Pig's head

The pig's head formation was shaped like a wedge. It was used to smash into an enemy line and push the men down with a wall of shields.

Tortoise

BEING BRAVE

There was a special standard called the *imago* with the emperor's face on it. This was meant to help soldiers feel strong and brave in fierce fighting.

BATTLE SIGNALS

A horn-player called a *cornicen* blew his horn to give signals to tell the soldiers what to do. For example, he might give the signal for soldiers to gather around their standard.

Standard-bearer holding the *imago*

Army horn-player (*cornicen*)

SIEGE!

When the Roman army invaded new lands it often found walled towns and fortresses that had to be conquered. Then there was a siege. The Romans surrounded the fortress and stopped the people getting food and supplies. Then the army attacked with special weapons, towers and ladders.

Ballista

Weapon swings on its stand

Arm springs up

Sling

Rock

Onager

⊙ ONAGER
The *onager* fired big rocks. Each rock was loaded into a sling on the end of an arm powered by twisted ropes.

⊙ BALLISTA
The *ballista* was a catapult used to fire shot or bolts (arrows). It could swing to aim.

⊙ CATAPULTA
A *catapulta* fired small bolts with iron tips. These could pierce the enemy soldiers' armour.

Winch draws back the bowstring

Catapulta

CLIMBING HIGH WALLS

The army built wooden towers, called siege towers, to get over high walls. They pushed them against the fortress and the soldiers climbed up inside. The wooden walls protected them from enemy missiles.

During long sieges, the Romans sometimes built huge ramps of wood, earth and stones to reach the top of walls.

Climbing heroes
The first soldier to climb an enemy's wall was given a gold crown and money. If he was killed, these went to his family.

ATTACK ON JOTAPATA

In CE 66, the Romans started a siege against the city of Jotapata in the Middle East. They used giant battering rams to crack the city walls.

The enemy poured boiling oil on them but in the end the Romans won and killed everyone. The Romans were often brutal after a siege, killing lots of townspeople.

AFTER THE BATTLE

Each legion had doctors to treat wounded soldiers on the battlefield. There was also a hospital in the fortress. The doctors knew which plants made good medicines. They grew some in the hospital's herb garden, and collected others. These were made into creams and potions.

 **AMPUTATIONS**
If a leg or an arm was badly injured it was usually amputated (cut off).

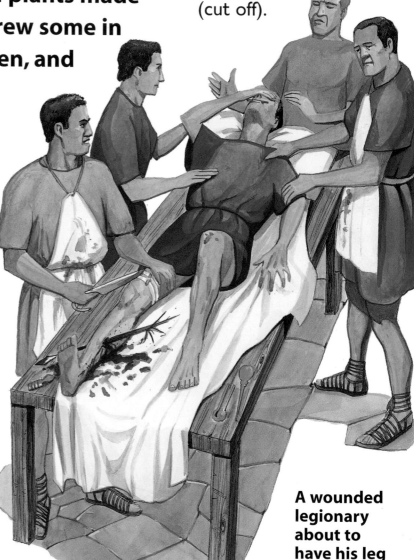

A wounded legionary about to have his leg amputated

FOR WOUNDS
The resin from a pine tree, called turpentine, was rubbed into soldiers' wounds to stop them becoming infected.

RELIEVING PAIN
The Romans did not have drugs to help someone having a very painful treatment such as an amputation. The doctor probably gave the patient lots of wine to dull the pain.

24

TRIUMPHAL MARCH

After a victory, legions sometimes paraded through Rome, cheered by huge crowds. They showed the treasure and prisoners that they had captured. The most important prisoner was executed (killed) in front of the crowd.

Victorious commander

Prisoners

Standard

Captured treasure

Emperor's worry
The legions were kept out of Rome in case they decided to revolt against the emperor.

THE EMPEROR'S GUARDS

The legions only went to Rome on triumphal marches. Usually, the only soldiers allowed inside Rome were the Praetorian Guard, who guarded the emperor. But sometimes the Praetorians turned against the emperor and murdered him.

GODS AND BELIEFS

The Romans believed in many gods and goddesses. If the gods were angry, terrible things could happen. To keep the gods happy, animals were sacrificed (killed) as offerings. The god of war was Mars. Before a battle, army commanders prayed to Mars and made sacrifices.

Statue of Mars

MARS WILL DECIDE

Soldiers believed that Mars decided who won, who lost and who died in battle. They prayed to him to ask him to keep them safe from harm and to allow them to win in battle.

Offerings to the gods

SACRIFICES

Romans sacrificed animals such as bulls, sheep and pigs. Then they asked the gods to help them by doing certain things. They wrote what they wanted on pieces of lead and threw them into underground streams and wells.

MITHRAISM

A religion from Persia called Mithraism was popular with soldiers. They sacrificed bulls to the god Mithras so that he would look after them if they died a violent death in battle. They did this in hidden underground temples.

Temples
People went to worship the gods in a temple. It had a raised place called an altar where sacrifices were made.

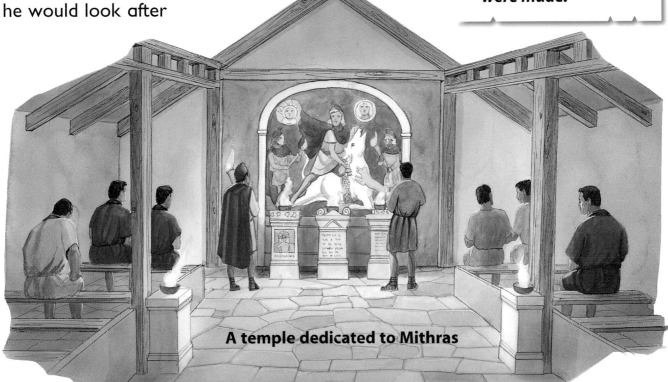

A temple dedicated to Mithras

BURIALS AND SUPERSTITIONS

Burial urn

Soldier's burial
A dead soldier was usually cremated (burned). His ashes were then buried in a jar called an urn.

Ashes pipe
Sometimes there was a pipe leading down to the urn. Family members could pour wine or oil down it as an offering.

Ashes pipe

Plaque to scare off evil spirits

Superstitions
Soldiers carried lucky charms and put plaques on walls to scare off evil spirits.

ᛤND ᛟF THᛤ ᛤMᛈIRᛤ

In CE 286, Emperor Diocletian split the Roman Empire into an eastern part and a western part.

In CE 410, barbarian invaders attacked Rome and the western Roman Empire collapsed. The eastern Empire became very important. Historians call it the Byzantine Empire. Its capital was the city of Constantinople. There are many remnants of the Roman Empire in our world today.

ROME IN RUINS
The invaders destroyed buildings and treasures.

CHRISTIANITY

The Bible in Latin

Church language
The Roman language, Latin, became the language of the Christian Church.

Emperor Justinian took power in CE 527

The old Roman alphabet

Emperor Constantine
Constantine became a Christian in about CE 312. He encouraged Romans to become Christians.

Eastern emperors
The rulers of the Byzantine Empire were Christian. They called themselves Holy Roman Emperors.

⚜ WHAT IS LEFT?

There are the remains of Roman fortresses and camps all over Europe and North Africa. Archaeologists have discovered equipment such as helmets, swords and pieces of armour. Many soldiers settled in the lands where they were serving. Their descendants may still live in those countries today. Perhaps you are one of them.

Scabbard

Legionary's helmet

Sword blade

Archaeological finds

Archaeology
The study of human history by examining ancient items that have been discovered, such as bones, the remains of buildings, weapons and possessions.

⚜ HADRIAN'S WALL

Emperor Hadrian ordered his men to build a wall across northern Britain in CE 121 to defend the frontier against the Scots and Picts who lived further north. It stretched for about 120 kilometres. You can still see it today. Soldiers patrolled the wall in armour, carrying javelins.

Hadrian's Wall

GLOSSARY

A date with "BCE" after it means "before the Common Era" (or "before the birth of Christ", also written as "BC"). A date with "CE" before it means "Common Era" (or "after the birth of Christ", also written as "AD").

Auxiliary
Soldier who was not a Roman citizen.

Battle formation
Lining up soldiers in a certain way when under attack or fighting.

A standard

Cavalry
Cavalrymen were soldiers who rode horses.

Centurion
Soldier of a legion in charge of a century (80 men).

Century
Group of 80 men who fought together. A centurion was in charge.

Cohort
Section of a legion containing 480 men. There were ten cohorts in each legion.

Conturbenium
A legion's smallest section. It was made up of eight men who lived, worked and fought together. The plural is conturbenia.

Cornicen
The legion's horn-player. Horns were used to make signals during battle.

Denarius
Roman coin. The plural is denarii.

Statue of the god Mars

Dynasty
Powerful rulers from the same family.

Empire
Group of states, countries or territories that were once independent (not controlled by another country or power), but now ruled by a single country or person.

Frontier or border
The boundary where the land of one country or power borders another.

Hand-to-hand combat
Fighting close up.

Hobnail
A short nail with a large head. It was used to protect the sole of sandals.

Imago
A special standard with the image of the emperor on it.

Legate
The man in command of a whole legion.

Legionary
Ordinary foot soldier.

Noble
Someone from an important family.

Oath
A promise. Soldiers had to take an oath (make a promise) to be loyal to the emperor.

Patrol
To move around an area to make sure it is safe, or to see what an enemy is doing.

Pension
Money that is saved while you are working so that you can live on it when you retire.

Roman citizen
A free Roman. Sometimes non-Romans were given Roman citizenship and this was a great honour.

Sentry
A soldier on guard duty.

Standard
Long pole with the legion's badges and symbols on it. In battle it was a meeting point for the soldiers.

Tribune
Legionary officer ranked below a legate. He came from a noble family.

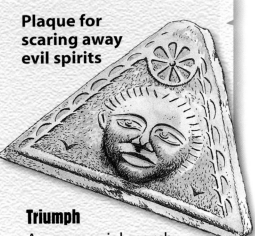

Plaque for scaring away evil spirits

Triumph
A ceremonial march through Rome, granted to legions when they won great campaigns.

Auxiliary foot soldier

Burial urn

INDEX